A+ books

Lions Are Awesome!

by Lisa J. Amstutz

Consultant: Jackie Gai, DVM
Captive Wildlife Veterinarian

CAPSTONE PRESS
a capstone imprint

A+ Books are published by Capstone Press,
1710 Roe Crest Drive, North Mankato, Minnesota 56003
www.capstonepub.com

Library of Congress Cataloging-in-Publication Data
Amstutz, Lisa J., author.
  Lions are awesome! / by Lisa J. Amstutz.
    pages cm. — (A+ books. Awesome African animals)
  Summary: "Describes the characteristics, habitat, behavior, life cycle, and threats to lions living
in the wild of Africa"—Provided by publisher.
  Audience: Ages 5–8.
  Audience: K to grade 3.
  Includes bibliographical references and index.
  ISBN 978-1-4914-1762-1 (library binding)
  ISBN 978-1-4914-1768-3 (paperback)
  ISBN 978-1-4914-1774-4 (eBook PDF)
1. Lion—Juvenile literature. 2. Animals—Africa—Juvenile literature. I. Title.

  QL737.C23A466 2015
  599.757—dc23   2014023671

Editorial Credits
Erika Shores and Mari Bolte, editors; Cynthia Della-Rovere, designer; Svetlana Zhurkin, media researcher;
Morgan Walters, production specialist

Photo Credits
Dreamstime: Robin Van Olderen, 12, SandraRBarba, 6—7, Smellme, 16 (right); Newscom: ZUMA Press/Tony
Crocetta, 26—27; Shutterstock: Aaron Amat, 27 (top), ala737, 13 (bottom), Alta Oosthuizen, 15 (top), 18, Ana
Gram, 25, 29 (inset), bjogroet, 11 (top), Black Sheep Media (grass), throughout, Chantal de Bruijne (African
landscape), back cover and throughout, creative, 10, e2dan, 13 (top), Eric Isselee, cover, back cover, 1, 4, 7 (top),
11 (bottom), 21 (top), 23 (top), 32, Gerrit_de_Vries, 14 (top), 17, Jez Bennett, 14 (bottom), John Michael Evan
Potter, 9, Maggy Meyer, 28—29, MattiaATH, 8, Mogens Trolle, 15 (bottom), moizhusein, 20—21, 23, Moments by
Mullineux, 5, Sean Stanton, 19, Serge Vero, 24, Stuart G. Porter, 22

Note to Parents, Teachers, and Librarians
This Awesome African Animals book uses full color photographs and a nonfiction format to introduce the
concept of lions. *Lions are Awesome!* is designed to be read aloud to a pre-reader or to be read independently by
an early reader. Photographs help listeners and early readers understand the text and concepts discussed. The
book encourages further learning by including the following sections: Table of Contents, Glossary, Read More,
Internet Sites, and Index. Early readers may need assistance using these features.

Printed in China by Nordica.
0914/CA21401520
092014   008470NORDS15

Table of Contents

Amazing Cats 4

Born to Hunt. 10

Lion Families 20

Staying Safe 26

Glossary 30

Read More 31

Internet Sites 31

Critical Thinking Using the Common Core . 31

Index. 32

Amazing Cats

Roar! The sound echoes across the plains. A lion's roar can be heard 5 miles (8 kilometers) away.

Lions are among the world's biggest cats. Males grow to about 8 feet (2.4 meters) long. They stand 4 feet (1.2 m) tall at the shoulder. Female lions are a little smaller.

A lion's fur is golden tan. It matches the dry grass of its African habitat. This helps hide the lion from its prey.

6

Male lions grow a long, shaggy mane. A mane makes them look bigger. It may also protect them in fights. Manes grow darker each year.

Most lions live in east-central and southern Africa. They roam open woodlands and grassy plains.

About 400 lions live in the Gir Forest of India. These lions are in danger of dying out.

Africa

Where Lions Live

Born to Hunt

Lions are carnivores. They hunt and kill other animals for food. Lions also steal food from other predators.

Hungry lions hunt large prey like antelope and zebras. They hunt smaller prey when other food is hard to find.

Lions hunt in groups. Females do most of the hunting, often at night. Lions see well in the dark. Their large eyes let in lots of light. Lions hear well too. Their ears turn to follow sound. They can hear prey 1 mile (1.6 km) away. Whiskers help lions find their way in the dark.

Lions walk about 5 miles (8 km) a day to find food. They sneak up on prey by hiding and waiting. Then they run and pounce.

A lion can eat up to
75 pounds (34 kilograms)
of meat in one day. That's
like 300 hamburgers!
Then it may not eat again
for a week.

Claws tip a lion's
toes. Lions scratch
them on trees. Then
they pull the claws
into their paws. This
keeps the claws sharp.

When a lion hunts, its front claws grab the prey. Its hind claws dig into the ground.

A lion's 30 sharp teeth tear meat from its prey. Lions have no flat teeth for chewing. So they gulp down chunks of meat.

Even a lion's tongue is made for eating meat. It is rough like sandpaper. Spiny bumps cover the surface. They scrape meat from bones.

Lion Families

A pride is a family of lions. Between 10 and 20 lions form a pride. Only a few are adult males. The rest are females and their young. They hunt together and share food.

The females care for each others' cubs. Males guard the territory where the pride lives and hunts. They mark this area with scent.

A female lion finds a mate when she is 3 years old. Soon one to six cubs are born. Each tiny cub weighs about 3 pounds (1.4 kg). The cubs are blind for the first few days. Their mother leaves them when she goes to find food. The cubs' spots hide them in the tall grass.

Cubs stay close to their mother for about two years. She feeds them milk at first. Soon they start eating meat.

The cubs like to play. Playing
together makes them strong and
teaches them how to hunt.

Staying Safe

Adult lions are too big for other animals to kill. Still they face many dangers. Diseases kill some lions. Leopards and hyenas can eat cubs.

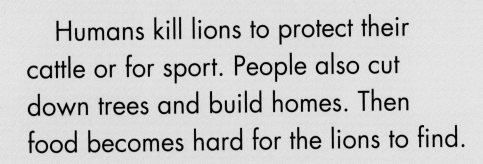

Humans kill lions to protect their cattle or for sport. People also cut down trees and build homes. Then food becomes hard for the lions to find.

In some areas where lions live, people have made parks called reserves. There no one can kill the lions. Fences keep lions from killing cattle or people. Tourists pay to see them in these reserves. With help from humans, this awesome "king of beasts" will always rule the land.

Glossary

carnivore (KAHR-nuh-vohr)—an animal that eats only meat

cub (kuhb)—a young lion

habitat (HAB-uh-tat)—the natural place and conditions in which a plant or animal lives

mane (MAYN)—long, thick hair that grows on the head and neck of some animals like lions and horses

plains (PLAYN)—a large, flat area of land with few trees

predator (PRED-uh-tur)—an animal that hunts other animals for food

prey (PRAY)—an animal hunted by another animal for food

pride (PRIDE)—a group of lions living together

reserve (ri-ZURV)—land that is protected so that animals may live there safely

territory (TER-uh-tor-ee)—the land on which an animal grazes or hunts for food, and raises its young

Read More

Franks, Katie. *Lions*. The Zoo's Who's Who. New York: PowerKids Press, 2015.

Ringstad, Arnold. *Lions*. Wild Cats. Mankato, Minn.: Amicus High Interest, 2014.

Zeiger, Jennifer. *Lions*. Nature's Children. New York: Children's Press, 2012.

Internet Sites

FactHound offers a safe, fun way to find Internet sites related to this book. All of the sites on FactHound have been researched by our staff.

Here's all you do:
Visit *www.facthound.com*
Type in this code: 9781491417621

 Check out projects, games and lots more at
www.capstonekids.com

Critical Thinking Using the Common Core

1. On page 29, the text says the lion is a "king of beasts." What do you think this name means? (Craft and Structure)

2. Look at all the pictures of lions hunting throughout the book. Would a lion without teeth and claws be a good hunter? Why or why not? (Integration of Knowledge and Ideas)

3. Describe how a lion's fur keeps it hidden. (Key Ideas and Details)

Index

claws, 16, 17

color, 6, 7, 22

cubs, 21, 22, 24, 25, 26

diseases, 26

family, 20

food, 10, 11, 15, 18, 19, 20, 22, 24, 27

fur, 6

Gir Forest, 8

hearing, 12

hunting, 10, 11, 12, 14, 17, 20, 21, 25

manes, 7

range, 8

reserves, 29

roar, 4

sight, 12

size, 5

teeth, 18

tongues, 19

whiskers, 12